REPTILES

Photo credits:

Chris McLaughlin/WaterHouse — Page 29
Rod Canham/WaterHouse — Page 7
Visuals Unlimited — Page 28
Joe McDonald/Visuals Unlimited — Pages 16, 19, 28
John Cunningham/Visuals Unlimited — Pages 13, 20, 28
R. Calentine/Visuals Unlimited — Pages 15, 29
Leonard L. Rue III/Visuals Unlimited — Page 28
Jim Merli/Visuals Unlimited — Pages 6, 13, 14, 20
David Matherly/Visuals Unlimited — Page 20
A. Kerstitch/Visuals Unlimited — Page 16
Tom J. Ulrich/Visuals Unlimited — Pages 11, 22
W.A. Banaszewski/Visuals Unlimited — Page 10
Don. W. Fawcett/Visuals Unlimited — Page 7
William Grenfell/Visuals Unlimited — Page 20
Walt Anderson/Visuals Unlimited — Page 8
Nathan W. Cohen/Visuals Unlimited — Pages 6, 14, 15
Photo Researchers — Page 12
Lawrence E. Naylor/Photo Researchers — Page 15
Francois Gohier/Photo Researchers — Page 29
Jeffrey W. Lang/Photo Researchers — Page 11
Tom McHugh/Photo Researchers — Pages 9, 13, 15, 18, 22–25
Stephen Dalton/Photo Researchers — Page 22
H.A. Thornhill/Photo Researchers — Page 12
J.H. Robinson/Photo Researchers — Page 17
Brian Enting/Photo Researchers — Page 23
Michael McCoy/Photo Researchers — Page 14
Gregory Dimijian/Photo Researchers — Page 13
Joyce Photographics/Photo Researchers — Page 7
R.W. Brooks/Photo Researchers — Page 21
Miguel Castro/Photo Researchers — Page 21
K.H. Switik/Photo Researchers — Pages 7, 20
Mark Picard/NE Stock Photo — Page 16
Art Phaeuf/NE Stock Photo — Page 18
Paul E. Clark/NE Stock Photo — Page 8
Thomas C. Boyden — Pages 10, 22
Anita Baskin-Salzberg — Pages 24, 27
Allen Salzberg — Pages 24, 27
Kit Kittle — Pages 7, 18, 19, 26
Lynn Rogers — Pages 12, 13, 24–27

End Pages — Photo Researchers

Illustrations:

Crystal Palette — Pages 17, 18, 25, 26, 27

Copyright ©1993
Kidsbooks, Inc.
3535 West Peterson Ave.
Chicago, IL 60659

EYES ON NATURE™

REPTILES

Written by
Robert Matero

kidsbooks® Incorporated

REMARKABLE REPTILES

Millions of years ago reptiles dominated the land, sea, and sky. Most of these ancient reptiles—including the dinosaurs—suddenly died out about 65 million years ago. No one knows exactly why. However, five different groups of their ancestors—snakes, crocodilians, lizards, turtles and tortoises, and the tuatara—about 6,500 different species in all, adapted to the changing world and survive today on every continent except Antarctica.

Sun Seekers

Reptiles have thick, scaly skin which prevents their bodies from drying out. The scales are made from keratin, the same material found in your fingernails and hair. The body temperature of these cold-blooded creatures depends on their surroundings. It goes up in warm weather and down in cold weather.

The heat from the sun warms the blood of this basking crocodile.

Shedding Skins

Most reptiles keep growing throughout their lives. Snakes and some lizards are able to shed their scaly outer layer of skin as they outgrow it. Lizard skin falls off in flakes but snakes shed their entire skin — sometimes unbroken—at one time.

Lots of Lizards

Lizards come in many sizes and colors, and some, like Jackson's chameleon, even have horns! A chameleon's eyes move independently of each other and in any direction. This allows it to search for food and avoid being eaten at the same time.

Turtles, crocodilians, and most snakes and lizards are hatched from eggs. Reptiles build nests of rotting plant material or dig holes in the warm sand or soil where they deposit their eggs. Some snakes and lizards are born live from eggs that hatch in their mother's body.

When they are ready to hatch, baby reptiles use a special pointed egg tooth or spike located on their snouts to chisel through the shell. Soon after, the egg tooth falls off. The hatchlings are identical to their parents—only smaller.

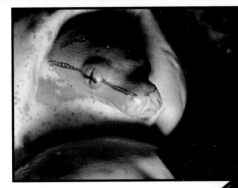

The Ancient One ▼

Lizard-like in appearance, the tuatara can trace its ancestors back to the time before dinosaurs roamed the Earth. The only survivors of this ancient group of reptiles live on a few islands near New Zealand.

Life In A Shell

The turtle's hard protective shell has enabled it to survive on Earth for over 250 million years. However, some sea turtles have developed a smoother, lighter, more streamlined shell, helping them to better adapt to life in the ocean.

CROCODILIANS

Alligators, crocodiles, gharials, and caimans belong to a group of reptiles known as crocodilians. They lived alongside the dinosaurs, but unlike them, crocodilians were able to adapt to the Earth's changes and survive.

Members of the crocodile family have long, sleek bodies covered with hard, bony scales that keep them well protected. They never stop growing and are thought by some to be the smartest of all reptiles.

Alligator

Crocodile Cousins

Alligators and crocodiles look very much alike. One way to tell them apart is by looking at their heads and jaws. An alligator has a rounded snout at the end of a slightly shorter head. A crocodile's head is longer and more triangular. When a crocodile closes its mouth, the larger teeth on its bottom jaw rest in spaces on the **outside** of its upper jaw. In an alligator's mouth, they rest on the **inside** of the jaw.

Crocodile

Caimans, living in Central and South America, are closely related to alligators. Alligators are found only in the southeastern part of the United States and in China.

Caiman

The Indian gharial has a long, slender snout and a bulb-like nose. Unlike other crocodilians, all of its sharp teeth—about 160 of them—are the same size. Gharials eat mainly fish and can grow to 20 feet. Though fierce-looking, the endangered gharial is really quite shy and timid.

8   Gharial

A Watery Life

Crocodilians are built for a life in and around water. They are strong swimmers — wiggling through the water with their powerful tails propelling them forward. When floating, the eyes, ears, and nostrils, positioned higher than the rest of the head, are exposed above the water. But when underwater, where they can remain for over an hour, transparent shields slide across their eyes to protect them.

Saltwater Crocodile

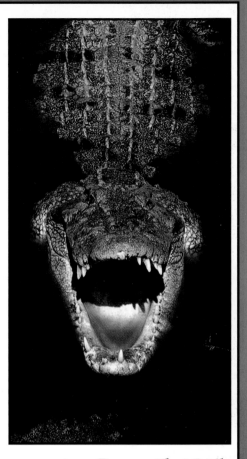

Beware That Smile

Silently gliding forward, eyes steady and riveted, the crocodile is a fearsome and aggressive hunter. It will attack large animals and is very dangerous to humans. Alligators, on the other hand, are shy. They will bite if disturbed but most likely will swim or run away when approached.

Record Breakers

Adult male crocodiles measuring over 14 feet are not uncommon, but the all-time champions of size are the saltwater crocodiles of southeast Asia which sometimes stretch out to more than 20 feet.

▶ This crocodile enjoys a peaceful float, but don't be fooled… he's got an eye out for any intruders.

Underwater Dining

Crocodilians cannot chew their food—they swallow it whole. If their prey is too large, they grab it with their sharp teeth, drag it underwater until it drowns, then rip it into chunks with powerful twists of their bodies. A throat flap keeps the water out of their lungs when diving, so they can swallow their food underwater.

A crocodile continually grows new sets of teeth to replace the ones lost while hunting. It can go through about fifty sets in a lifetime!

Powerful Jaws

With one snap an alligator's jaws are powerful enough to cut a large animal in two. However, the muscles which open its mouth are so weak that once shut the alligator's mouth can easily be held together.

All crocodilians are flesh eaters and feed on any animals they can catch — from birds and fish to zebras or antelope. Gharials eat mainly fish. Some crocodilians swallow small stones which help to grind their food and also enable them to float low in the water.

Lazy Day ▶

Much of this crocodile's day is spent basking in the warm sun. At dusk it will perk up and begin hunting for its dinner.

Alligator Nest

This crocodile is not eating her eggs. Her babies are ready to be born and she's gently rubbing the shells so that they may be released.

Squeak! A saltwater ▶ crocodile, 12 inches long and weighing five ounces, emerges from its shell. As an adult it can measure 20 feet and weigh as much as 2,000 pounds.

Nests and Babies

Female crocodiles dig a hole into which they deposit their eggs in two or three layers before covering them with sand. Alligators prepare rounded nests of mud and decaying vegetation above the ground. Both nests protect the eggs as the sun's warmth incubates them. Unlike most other reptiles, crocodilian mothers guard their nests and stay close to their babies after they are born.

◀ A mother alligator carries her babies to the water on her back—sometimes in her mouth—as carefully as a mother dog carries her puppies. The hatchlings are miniature versions of their parents.

SNAKES...

Although lacking legs, eyelids, and outer ears, snakes have managed to survive and prosper for over 135 million years. About 2,700 species of snakes are alive today. Multi-patterned and colored, snakes make their homes on land, in water, underground, and in trees.

New Skin

A snake is not slimy—its scaly skin is dry and smooth. The outer layer of a snake's skin cannot stretch, so when a snake grows too big for its skin it simply develops a new one. This blue racer has broken through its old skin and will soon crawl out with shiny new scales.

Snakes are not vegetarians. They prefer to dine on birds, lizards, mammals, other snakes, frogs, eggs, earthworms, and insects. By unhinging its jaws, a snake is able to swallow large prey—larger than the size of its mouth.
◀This slender garter snake has hunted down a toad, which has puffed itself up to try to prevent from being swallowed.

◄ Sensitive Tongues
A snake flicks out its long, forked tongue to touch and smell. This viper uses its sensitive tongue to scan the area for prey. A snake can follow a scent very well— smelling with its tongue.

Unusual Mother ▼
A python lays between 15 and 100 eggs and is the only snake that helps them hatch. By coiling around her eggs and vibrating her body, this Indian python not only protects them, but keeps the eggs warm and speeds up the hatching.

▲The common garter snake is found throughout the United States. Unlike most snakes, garter babies are born live, usually in litters of 50 to 60.

◄ Camouflage
A snake's color and scale pattern helps it to blend in with its surroundings. The beautiful coloring of this emerald tree boa helps camouflage it from both predator and prey amongst the leafy canopy of the South American rain forest.

▶

These eastern hognosed snakes have chiseled through their leathery shells with their egg teeth. However, in no hurry to enter the world, they will stay inside the safety of their shells for a day or two before crawling out.

Born to Swim
All snakes can swim and some have chosen to live at sea rather than on land. Sea snakes thrive in the warm waters of the Indian and Pacific Oceans and are extremely poisonous. These swift swimmers can stay underwater for several hours before coming up for air. Sea snake babies are born live at sea.

...AND MORE SNAKES

Most snakes are non-poisonous. They capture their meals by suffocating their prey or by simply biting and gripping them with their sharp teeth. Then, snakes use their large, extended mouths and flexible bodies to swallow their victims. Snakes do not chew — they swallow their food whole and slowly digest it. After a large meal, a snake can go for many months without eating again.

These tree boas aren't having a conversation. They're just hanging out on their favorite branches. Heat sensors along their lips help them detect the tree-dwelling prey on which they feed.

Giant Snake

Constrictors are thick, long, and heavy. South American anacondas easily grow longer than 20 feet and weigh over 500 pounds. One huge anaconda measured 28 feet and weighed in at an incredible 1,100 pounds. This constrictor could swallow a jaguar — whole!

Deadly Embrance

Boas, pythons, and anacondas are constrictors — snakes that suffocate their prey. After seizing a bird in its jaws, this diamond python wraps its body around it and slowly tightens the coils each time the bird exhales. Soon the bird can no longer breathe and finally dies. The constrictor then swallows it whole, digesting everything except the feathers.

14

▲ Patience

On a branch high above the ground, this slender Central American vine snake tries to imitate a tree limb. A vine snake can stay perfectly still for hours, hoping to fool a bird or lizard into thinking it's just another vine...until, gulp! it's too late to get away.

Look Alikes ▶

The harmless scarlet king snake's unusual coloring makes it look like the deadly coral snake. But remember: "Red touches black, venom lack. Red touches yellow, kills a fellow."

Coral Snake   King Snake

◀ Egg Snatcher

An egg-eating snake can stretch its mouth very wide and slowly move its jaws over an egg. It can swallow eggs twice as wide as its body! Sharp bones in the snake's throat crack and crush the egg, allowing it to swallow the liquid part and spit out the shell.

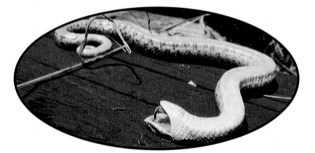

▲ The Great Pretender

Upon encountering an enemy, the harmless hognosed snake puffs out its neck, hisses, and pretends to strike. If this act fails, it turns over onto its back and plays dead.

Big Ball ▼

When threatened, the African ball python tucks in its head and coils itself into a tight, round ball, which incredibly, can be rolled... but not bounced!

15

DEADLY FANGS

Of the approximately 800 poisonous snakes, about 250 are dangerous to humans. When a poisonous snake bites, special glands pump venom through its hollow fangs and inject the poison into its victim.

◄ The muscular body of the rare, yellow eyelash viper helps it move easily through the dense tropical forest. Tree-dwelling snakes drink the moisture that collects on leaves.

Venomous Vipers

A viper keeps its extra-long fangs folded back against the roof of its mouth—until it's ready to strike. Vipers have wide heads in which they store their large venom glands. Gaboon vipers, found in tropical African forests, have the longest fangs— up to two inches—of any snake.

Gaboon Viper

Pit Vipers

Some vipers have pits — small holes—one on either side of their faces. These heat-sensing organs help the viper locate prey, especially at night.

▼ The best known pit viper is the rattlesnake. The rattle on the end of its tail is made up of dry, hard pieces of unshed skin. When shaken, the rattle makes a whirring, buzzing sound, warning strangers to stay away.

Can you guess why I'm called a rhinoceros viper?

Copperhead ▲
The copperhead's markings allow it to blend in with the dead leaves on the forest floor. Although painful, this pit viper's bite is rarely fatal to humans.

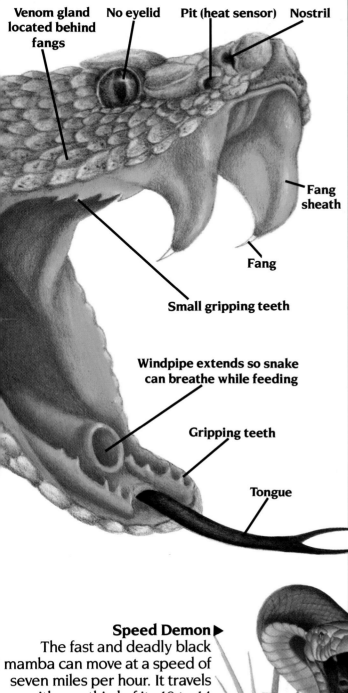

Venom gland located behind fangs

No eyelid

Pit (heat sensor)

Nostril

Fang sheath

Fang

Small gripping teeth

Windpipe extends so snake can breathe while feeding

Gripping teeth

Tongue

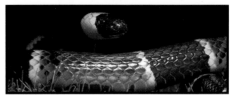

Coral Snake

Fixed Fangs

Unlike vipers, the colorful coral snake, along with its cobra, mamba, and sea snake relatives, has two short, sharp fangs fixed at the front end of its upper jaw.

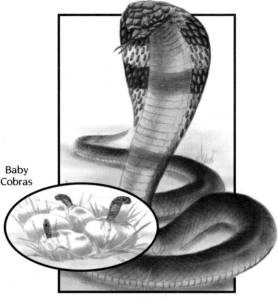

Baby Cobras

Hooded Terror ▲

The 18-foot king cobra is the longest poisonous snake in the world, with venom powerful enough to kill an elephant. When threatened, it spreads the loose skin on its neck into a "hood" several times wider than its body. Moving with its upper body raised off the ground, a hooded cobra is indeed a fearsome sight!

Aggressive baby cobras, armed with fangs and venom, will strike while still emerging from their shells.

Speed Demon ▶

The fast and deadly black mamba can move at a speed of seven miles per hour. It travels with one third of its 10 to 14 foot-long body lifted off the ground and can strike at the level of a person's head. Just two drops of venom from this African snake can kill a human in ten minutes!

Lizards

With over 3,500 different species, lizards are by far the largest group of reptiles. They range in size from an inch-long gecko to the 10 foot-long Komodo dragon, and come in many shapes and colors.

Australian Blue-Tongued Skink

Tree-dwelling Chameleon

Sensitive Tongues

Lizards extend or flick their tongues to help them "sense" their environment. The information gathered tells them the whereabouts of food and mates, and warns them of the presence of enemies. But their tongues have other uses, too.

A tree-dwelling chameleon is the "marksman" of the reptile world. Its tongue, kept rolled up in its mouth, is as long or longer than its body. When the chameleon spots an insect, it shoots its sticky tongue out, and zap! — instant lunch.

The Australian blue-tongued skink sticks out and waves its fat blue tongue to frighten away its enemies.

◀ Geckos use their long tongues to clean their faces — including their eyes.

Masters of Disguise

Many lizards have a well known ability to change color. They can match their surroundings to hide from both prey and predator. But first prize for color change goes to the chameleon, who can even change its color to suit its mood.

This chameleon has no trouble blending in with the sunlit foliage of its east African home.

Natural Camouflage

Touch this branch and you've moved an almost-impossible-to-detect giant gecko.

A Tale Of Tails

Many lizards possess the amazing ability to shed their tails when attacked. Incredibly, the dropped tail keeps wriggling, distracting the enemy and giving the lizard a chance to escape. But the lost tail is not missed for long because a lizard can grow another one! Sometimes, if only part of the tail has come off, a lizard, like this skink above, will wind up with two tails.

The bright blue tail of a young skink below draws an enemy's attention away from its body. Better to lose your tail than your life!

Worm? Or Lizard?

Lizards without legs look a lot like small snakes — or huge worms. The worm lizard spends most of its time underground where legs aren't necessary. Moving forward or backward, it hunts for insects and, you guessed it, worms.

◀ Heads Or Tails?

The shingleback or double-headed lizard of Australia really has only one head. But its fat, head-shaped tail makes it look like it has two. This confuses its enemies and, hopefully, causes them to attack the wrong end.

Leopard Gecko

Eggs and Babies

Like their snake cousins, some lizards are born live, but most mothers simply lay their eggs and walk away.

This female leopard gecko had just laid her eggs in a shallow nest. The eggs, soft and sticky, will harden during the months they take to hatch.

Its mother long gone, this green iguana emerges from its leathery shell, ready to fend for itself.

▼ The female North American five-lined skink is one of the few lizards that guards its eggs and cares for its young until they can survive on their own.

Iguana Iguana

Iguanas, the most common lizards living in Central and South America, come in many shapes, sizes, and colors. They live in forests and deserts, and one species has even adapted to saltwater living.

Some iguanas like to live in groups, and it is not uncommon to see groups of 40 to 50 sunning themselves.

▲ These green, ring-tailed iguanas have found a rock to rest on in the South American forest.

◄ The rhinoceros iguana, with tiny horns on its snout, looks like a fierce mini-dinosaur. In captivity, however, it is peaceful and friendly.

20

◄Gila Monster

The poisonous gila monster is too slow to chase down its dinner, so it feeds on eggs and new-born baby animals. Extra food is stored as fat in its thick tail, so a gila can live for more than a year without eating.

Frilled Lizard

The Australian frilled lizard spends most of its life in trees. However, if cornered on the ground, it rears on its back legs, extends the enormous frill around its head, opens its mouth wide, and *hissss-es* away.

Diving Iguanas

The marine iguana of the Galapagos Islands, 600 miles off the coast of South America, is the only lizard that has adapted to saltwater living. It can dive as deep as 30 feet to find the seaweed it likes to eat. After it leaves the cold water, the iguana climbs back on the rocks to bask in the hot sun.

Plumed Basilisk

Walking On Water

The basilisk of Central and South America can actually run on water! Taking advantage of its extra-long back feet and super speed, this lizard can go several strides before its lightweight body sinks in.

Plumed basilisks have sail-like crests that extend the full length of their bodies.

"Gek-oh, Gek-oh"

Chirping that sound is how the gecko got its name. These fascinating lizards are welcome visitors in many Asian homes. In addition to gobbling gobs of insects, some consider them a sign of good luck.

Geckos are wonderful climbers. The soft pads of the underside of their feet are equipped wth tiny, brush-like hooks. The hooks enable them to hang upside down on ceilings and cling to glass.

Some geckos can fly, too! By spreading an extra flap of skin along its body, the tiny flying gecko glides across the ▶ jungle treetops of Asia.

▼ West Indian Spotted Gecko

One Of A Kind ▲

Once mistaken for a lizard, the tuatara is the only remaining member of an entire group of ancient reptiles. The Maori people of New Zealand gave the tuatara its name, which means "peaks on the back."

The tuatara's skull is very strong and similar to that of a crocodile. Sharing a burrow with sea birds, the tuatara spends the hottest part of the day there, emerging at night to hunt for food. It can remain active at much colder temperatures than other reptiles.

Life begins slowly for the tuatara. It takes between twelve and fifteen months for its eggs to hatch, longer than any other reptile. Life is long, too, usually lasting over 100 years.

22

Spiked Defense ▼

Horned toads are small lizards with toadlike faces. Their bodies are covered with pointed spines and large "horns" which are extremely sharp. When frightened, a horned toad will sometimes squirt little streams of blood from the corners of its eyes.

Horned
Toad

◄ Giant Lizard

Weighing as much as 350 pounds, the fierce Komodo dragon is the largest living lizard. It preys on large animals such as deer and wild boar, and has been known to attack and kill humans. When feeding, this lizard's jaws work so hard that it needs four new sets of teeth each year. Komodo dragons are only found on a few small Indonesian islands.

One of the tuatara's most interesting features is the third "eye," located on the top of its brain. Although skin covers the eye, it remains sensitive to light, but is unable to "see" images like a true eye.

23

TORTOISES AND TURTLES

Giant Tortoise

About 250 species of turtles and tortoises— the only reptiles with shells—inhabit the warmer areas of the Earth. The turtle's shell system has protected it so well that turtles have lived on Earth, practically unchanged, for about 200 million years.

Diamondback Terrapin

When this painted turtle feels threatened, it tucks itself into its "home" until the danger passes. ▼

Green Sea Turtle

What's in a name?
The name turtle usually refers to animals that live in freshwater—lakes, rivers, ponds, and streams. Sea turtles live in the ocean. Turtles that spend most or all of their time on land are called tortoises. Terrapin, a native American word meaning "little turtle," refers to small freshwater turtles, in particular the diamondback terrapin.

Carapace

Plastron

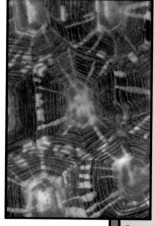

◄ Either a layer of tough leathery skin, or hard plates called scutes [scoots] cover the shell. Each species has its own scute pattern which keeps getting larger as the turtle grows.

Scute Pattern

Shell System
The turtle's shell is part of its skeleton. The shell is made up of two parts, the curved upper part (carapace) and the flattish lower part (plastron).

Clever and Deadly

Although toothless, this American snapping turtle is ready to use its strong, sharp beak to deliver a vicious bite. The snapper prefers to live in quiet muddy streams and ponds where it can snap away at fish, frogs, and water birds.

The alligator snapping turtle lies camouflaged in the mud with its mouth open. The turtle wriggles a worm-like pink flap on its tongue to lure small fish inside its deadly jaws.

Instead of teeth, turtles have beak-like jaws which snap and chop plants and small animals into bite-sized pieces. On land, turtles feed mainly on slow-moving prey, such as insects and worms. Many eat plants, too. Tortoises are vegetarians.

Loose fringes of skin dangle from the neck and head of the South American matamata turtle. Mistaking the fringes for worms, fish are lured close to its jaws. Suddenly, the strange-looking matamata opens wide and sucks in its dinner!

25

◄ Soft Shell

Turtles that spend most of their lives in freshwater tend to have lighter, flatter shells than land turtles. Instead of hard, horny plates, the streamlined body of this spiny soft-shelled turtle is covered by leathery skin.

Boxed In

The eastern box turtle lives in damp fields and forests. When threatened, a hinge on its plastron (underside) allows it to tuck itself tightly into its protective shell.

Long Distance Travelers

▲ Some green sea turtles migrate over 2,000 miles across the Atlantic Ocean to lay their eggs on the same beach on which they were born. Weighing less than an ounce, these babies all hatch together and quickly dash to the safety of the sea.

A swimming sea turtle is the world's fastest reptile. Its lightweight, streamlined shell and strong, flat flippers help propel the sea turtle through the ocean at speeds up to 20 mph.

◄ Old Timers

Galapagos tortoises can grow up to four feet in shell length and weigh as much as 600 pounds. These land giants have strong thick legs to support their weight. Tortoises live longer than any other animal — some have lived more than 150 years!

Basking Together ►

A group of painted turtles bask under the warm sun. Like all reptiles, cold-blooded turtles need the sun's warmth to raise their blood temperature. Painted turtles, the most numerous small turtles in North America, like to bask in groups.

Turtle Tears ▶

This tearful loggerhead sea turtle isn't sad because she's leaving over 100 of her eggs on shore. She may have gotten sand in her eyes when she covered her nest, or she's simply "crying" away the extra salt she swallowed swimming in the salty ocean.

Green Sea Turtle

Giant

The leatherback sea turtle is by far the largest of all turtles—on land or in the sea. Weighing up to 2,000 pounds, this giant can dive almost three-quarters of a mile before coming up for air. Instead of a hard, rigid shell, the leatherback is covered with tough, leathery skin.

Leatherback Turtle

▲This mother-to-be is laying her eggs into a recently dug nest. All turtles, even those who live in the sea, lay eggs on land—although never far from water. Turtles do not take care of their eggs or babies. The sun's warmth or heat created by rotting vegetation keeps the eggs warm until they hatch.

A newly hatched eastern box turtle.

27

SNAKE ROUNDUP

"Dancing" Rattlers ▶

During mating season, male rattlesnakes will engage in a kind of combat "dance." They wave their bodies, trying to frighten each other away by displaying their size and strength.

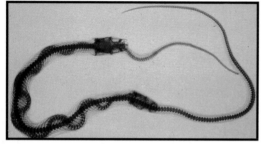

▲ Snakes have long, flexible spines containing between 200 and 400 bones, depending on size. A pair of ribs is attached to each bone supporting the strong muscles needed to move swiftly and swallow large prey. This x-ray reveals the bodies of two snakes — one in the process of swallowing the other!

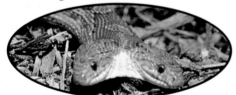

▲ Double Trouble

As strange as it is rare, sometimes a two-headed snake is born. This can be a real problem if it happens to be a snake-eating snake because one head may attack and try to swallow the other!

▲ Snake Milk?
People "milk" snakes to get their venom. The venom is used to make an antitoxin to help cure snakebites.

▲ A cobra cannot hear nor dance to the music of this swaying snake-charmer's flute. Instead, it follows his movements.

With no outer ears, snakes do not "hear." Instead, bones in their bodies feel and carry vibrations from the ground to inner ears in their skulls.

ENDANGERED REPTILES

Reptiles, like all other animals, contribute to the variety and beauty of life in their own special way. Today, many reptiles, for a variety of reasons, are endangered. The greatest threat comes from humans. As human population increases, the need for land grows, changing an animal's natural environment. Pollution at sea and on land also contributes to loss of habitat, and life.

▲ Demand for the skin of crocodilians, lizards, and snakes to make belts, wallets, shoes, handbags, and other leather goods has seriously threatened many species. About 20 members of the crocodile family, including this Brazilian caiman, are listed as endangered species.

The hawksbill sea turtle is in danger of extinction. Its beautiful shell is used for making jewelry and ornaments.

◀ Many snakes, like these rattlesnakes, are needlessly killed each year because of people's fear of them.

▲
Success Story
Once endangered, the American alligator has made a strong comeback due to protection policies.